"A good set of character Bible studies is hard to find. The ORDINARY GREATNESS series is a solid tool for spiritual growth."

— DARRELL BOCK, research professor of New Testament Studies, professor of spiritual development and culture, Dallas Theological Seminary

"Many studies of biblical characters are designed to inspire and encourage, but this one aims at something different: transformation. By continually driving us back to God's Word and pointing us to the person of Jesus, the ORDINARY GREATNESS series provides the perfect antidote to the boredom and inward focus of our day."

— JOHN DYER, ThM, author of *From the Garden to the City*

"ORDINARY GREATNESS is a series that invites people to know the Word of God thoroughly, interpret it accurately, and apply it passionately. This is a key resource for anyone looking to break new ground in their knowledge of the Bible and their intimacy with the Lord."

— TIMOTHY ATEEK, director, Vertical Ministries

"Change is inevitable, but the right kind of change is special. God is the agent of lasting change in our lives. This series will help identify the changes God wants to make in you by showing you the changes He has made in biblical heroes. Blake, Matt, and Brian can lead you well because they have been led themselves by the Lord."

— GREGG MATTE, pastor, Houston's First Baptist Church; founder, Breakaway Ministries

"Our twenty-first-century popular culture seems to ignore the need for rock-solid character growth. Blake, Matt, and Brian take us on a journey with three very human biblical men — Daniel, Gideon, and Peter — and show us how they grew into giants of the faith. This well-crafted series brings the Bible alive through lots of Scripture, opportunities for self-discovery, relevant stories, and a bias toward application."

— KEN COCHRUM, vice president, student-led and virtually led movements, Cru

BLAKE JENNINGS
MATT MORTON
BRIAN FISHER

# PETER

## FROM RECKLESS TO ROCK SOLID

TH1NK, an
Imprint of
NavPress

NavPress is the publishing ministry of The Navigators, an international Christian organization and leader in personal spiritual development. NavPress is committed to helping people grow spiritually and enjoy lives of meaning and hope through personal and group resources that are biblically rooted, culturally relevant, and highly practical.

**For a free catalog go to www.NavPress.com**
**or call 1.800.366.7788 in the United States or 1.800.839.4769 in Canada.**

© 2012 by Blake Jennings, Matthew Morton, and Brian Fisher

ISBN-13: 978-1-61291-145-8
ISBN-13: 978-1-61291-423-7 (electronic)

Cover design by Arvid Wallen

Some of the anecdotal illustrations in this book are true to life and are included with the permission of the persons involved. All other illustrations are composites of real situations, and any resemblance to people living or dead is coincidental.

Unless otherwise identified, all Scripture quotations in this publication are taken from the *Holy Bible, New International Version*® (NIV®). Copyright © 1973, 1978, 1984 by Biblica, used by permission of Zondervan, all rights reserved. Other versions used include: *THE MESSAGE* (MSG). Copyright © 1993, 1994, 1995, 1996, 2000, 2001, 2002. Used by permission of NavPress Publishing Group; The Holy Bible, English Standard Version (ESV), copyright © 2001 by Crossway Bibles, a division of Good News Publishers. Used by permission. All rights reserved; and the New American Standard Bible® (NASB), copyright © 1960, 1962, 1963, 1968, 1971, 1972, 1973, 1975, 1977, 1995 by The Lockman Foundation. Used by permission.

Printed in the United States of America

1 2 3 4 5 6 7 8 / 17 16 15 14 13 12

# Contents

Acknowledgments 7

How to Use This Study 9

Lesson 1: Divinity in Disguise 13

Lesson 2: Your Mission, Should You Choose to Accept It 23

Lesson 3: Faith and Fear in a Fury 33

Lesson 4: Two Steps Forward, Two Steps Back 43

Lesson 5: The Last Are First 53

Lesson 6: Epic Fail 63

Lesson 7: Gracious Save 73

Lesson 8: A New Man 85

Leader's Guide 97

Notes 107

About the Authors 109

# Acknowledgments

WE WOULD LIKE to thank the many people who helped us complete this Bible study. Thank you to our wives, who supported and encouraged us during a frenetic year of simultaneous preaching and writing. Thank you to the wonderful elders and staff of Grace Bible Church, who gave us the time to write. And special thanks to Alyssa Luff, our research assistant for this study.

# How to Use This Study

A YOUNG, UNEDUCATED fisherman named Simon longed to become someone great, a man people knew, respected, and admired. Fortunately for him, God desired the same thing—to make him great. But great at what? What does it really mean for a person to be great? Like most young people, Simon assumed that greatness could be found in fame, popularity, success, wealth, and personal achievement. But God's path to greatness led Simon in a very different direction—through weakness, selflessness, humiliation, sacrifice, and ultimately, death. Through that humbling journey, God transformed Simon, the ambitious fisherman, into Peter the rock, the leader of Christ's church, and one of the greatest men the world has ever known. That's the awe-inspiring irony of Peter's story. Only by trading his own selfish ambitions for the selfless ambitions of his Savior could he become a man so great that people continue to study and follow his example two thousand years later!

We hope that this study of Peter's life will inspire, challenge, and equip you to discover the path to true, lasting greatness found only in Jesus Christ. In Peter's story we get to see the radical transformation that God the Son and God the Spirit can bring about in the life of a believer. Even for those of us who've failed miserably in the past, Peter's life proves that God can and will use us to change the world in amazing ways if we're willing to follow the example of His Son.

Studying God's Word has the potential to transform us in amazing ways if we approach it with obedient hearts and open minds. The best environment for any Bible study is a small group of friends with whom you can discuss the questions and passages. We learn best when we have other people to encourage us and to hold us accountable. If you do this study with a group, answer the questions on your own throughout the week and then get together with your friends to discuss what you have learned and to encourage one another to live it out.

Each lesson is divided into four main sections. First, you will find some introductory comments, the lesson's primary Bible passage, and two or three questions designed to get you thinking about the relevant topic for that week. The second section, called "Look It Over," will ask you to make some basic observations about the week's Bible passage. Third, "Think It Through" will take you a bit deeper into questions about the passage's meaning for the original audience and its relevance for us. Finally, "Make It Real" will challenge you to apply the passage to your own life. Throughout the lessons you'll find one or two personal download applications. You'll be able to recognize them by the following download icon. Try not to skip these activities because they'll challenge you to really examine yourself and the main points of the week. At the end of each lesson there is a memory verse, chosen so that you can keep the main point of the lesson on your heart and mind throughout the week. If you are short on time one week, ask your leader which portions of the study will be most valuable for the group discussion.

You'll notice that every lesson includes the full text of the main Scripture reading(s), but you'll want to have a Bible or Bible app handy to look up the additional passages referenced throughout the lessons. Be sure to bring your Bible to your group meeting so you can discuss these passages with your friends.

We hope that you enjoy this study and that it is a useful tool as you grow in your understanding and application of God's Word. If you would like more information about Bible study methods or would like

to download some additional curriculum, check us out online at www
.grace-bible.org.

*Blake Jennings, Matt Morton, and Brian Fisher*

# Divinity in Disguise

God exalted him to the highest place and gave him the name that is above every name, that at the name of Jesus every knee should bow, in heaven and on earth and under the earth, and every tongue confess that Jesus Christ is Lord, to the glory of God the Father.

PHILIPPIANS 2:9-11

IN JANUARY 2007, in the L'Enfant subway station of Washington, D.C., a young man in cheap clothing took up a spot next to a trashcan and pulled out a violin. He put his case out to collect tips, and began to play during the morning rush hour. In most metro areas, there's nothing unusual about that scene: struggling street musicians trying to earn a few bucks while the masses pass by. But this particular man *was* unusual. This was Joshua Bell, possibly the greatest violinist in the world. He typically earns $1,000 *per minute* for his performances. And he didn't play any average tune that day. He played Bach's Chaconne, one of the most difficult pieces ever written for the violin. And he played it on a Stradivarius, a violin worth $3.5 million! So one of the greatest musicians in the world stood in a subway station playing one of the hardest compositions ever written on one of the most expensive instruments ever built. Can you imagine the response he got from those who passed by? It wasn't what you might expect. Of the 1,097 people who passed him while he played that piece, only twenty of them stopped to give him a tip. Most people didn't even pause; they didn't even look at him![1]

Why? Why did so few people notice greatness when it was standing right in front of them? They failed to recognize Bell's greatness because it was not "packaged" as they expected. He wasn't dressed well. He wasn't playing in a concert hall. He did not look the part.

Peter's first encounter with Jesus began with the same mistake. Even though Jesus was and is the King of kings and the only Son of God, He didn't look the part. And yet sometimes Jesus pulled back the veil just a bit to let a person like Peter see past His humble exterior to the almighty power of God that resided within Him. Read Luke 5:1-11:

> One day as Jesus was standing by the Lake of Gennesaret, with the people crowding around him and listening to the word of God, he saw at the water's edge two boats, left there by the fishermen, who were washing their nets. He got into one of the boats, the one belonging to Simon, and asked him to put out a little from shore. Then he sat down and taught the people from the boat.
>
> When he had finished speaking, he said to Simon, "Put out into deep water, and let down the nets for a catch."
>
> Simon answered, "Master, we've worked hard all night and haven't caught anything. But because you say so, I will let down the nets."
>
> When they had done so, they caught such a large number of fish that their nets began to break. So they signaled their partners in the other boat to come and help them, and they came and filled both boats so full that they began to sink.
>
> When Simon Peter saw this, he fell at Jesus' knees and said, "Go away from me, Lord; I am a sinful man!" For he and all his

companions were astonished at the catch of fish they had taken, and so were James and John, the sons of Zebedee, Simon's partners.

Then Jesus said to Simon, "Don't be afraid; from now on you will catch men." So they pulled their boats up on shore, left everything and followed him.

»»»»»»»»»»»»»»»»»»»»»»»»»»»»»»»»»»»»»»»»»»»»»»»»»»»»»»»»

## FROM FISHING TO FOLLOWING

To understand this encounter between Jesus and Peter on the Lake of Gennesaret, we need a little background on fishing in first-century Israel. Gennesaret, also known as the Sea of Galilee, supported a profitable fishing industry that supplied much of Israel. Though not wealthy, commercial fishermen were well-trained, made a decent living, and had good standing in the community. They were what we would call "middle class," especially those who owned and operated their own boats as Peter and his partners did. That's what makes Peter's decision to simply abandon his business and career so stunning.[2]

# FACE-TO-FACE WITH THE ALMIGHTY

1. Has God ever done something amazing, even miraculous, in your own life to demonstrate His power? What did He do? How did you respond?

2. How do you think you would feel if you saw Jesus face-to-face? What would you say or do? Why?

3. Do you think we should feel fear toward God? Why or why not?

## A HUMBLING ENCOUNTER

Seminary students at my alma mater in Dallas don't receive many perks, with one glaring exception: membership in the Tom Landry Center, the best equipped and most prestigious gym in the city. Thanks to Landry's generous heart and Christian faith, seminary students are always welcome at his gym. They enjoy state-of-the-art weight-lifting equipment, cardio machines, racquetball courts, an indoor track, and even an Olympic-size pool. Because of the gym's outstanding reputation, students even get to rub shoulders with professional athletes from time to time. I (Blake) will never forget the day that the entire Boston Celtics basketball team walked by while I was changing in the locker room. I have never felt so small! I'm five foot ten, exactly the average height for an American male, yet I didn't even come up to the shoulders of their tallest players. Every non-Celtic man in the locker room stared awestruck as these giants walked through.

We often go through our daily lives feeling confident and capable, at least in the areas of life at which we excel, whether academics, athletics, music, our jobs, or our social lives. Occasionally, though, we have an experience that humbles us and makes us feel small, like my encounter with the Boston Celtics. Peter felt confident in his own area of expertise:

fishing. He was part-owner of a sizable fishing fleet. He knew the waters of the Sea of Galilee like the back of his hand. Through fishing, he was able to support his family. He seemed to have his life together.

>>>>>>>>>>>>>>>>>>>>>>>>>>>>>>>>>>>>>>>>>>>>>>>>>>>>>>>>>>>>>>>>>>>>>>>>>>

### AN ABSURD REQUEST

Peter's stunning act (leaving his fishing business) came as a result of an even more stunning miracle. After a long night of fruitless toil, a carpenter-turned-preacher with no fishing experience arrived and told these professional fishermen to get back into their boats, lower their freshly cleaned nets, and fish in the bright light of day when the fish could easily see and avoid their nets in the clear waters of Galilee. Jesus' request was absurd — no one could catch fish with a net in the daytime! But the impossibility of the request made the catch all the more miraculous and convinced these professionals that Jesus was a man worth following.[3]

But then Jesus arrived, got into Peter's boat, and turned his world upside down. In the events described in Luke 5, Peter experienced an encounter far more humbling than my encounter with the Boston Celtics. Seeing Jesus' power revealed to Peter how small and in need of help he really was.

## LOOK IT OVER

4. Examine Luke 5:1-11 carefully. What key words and ideas seem particularly important in order to understand the story? Summarize the main point of the passage in your own words.

   a. Key words:

b. Key ideas:

c. Main idea:

5. According to the passage, how did Peter feel when Jesus asked him to cast out his nets? Did this seem reasonable or wise to Peter? Why or why not?

6. How did Peter's opinion of Jesus change through this event? In other words, what did he think about Jesus at the beginning of the passage, and what did he think about Jesus at the end of the passage?

## THINK IT THROUGH

7. What did Peter mean when he called himself "sinful"? For help, read Romans 3:9-12 and 3:23.

8. Why did Peter become afraid of Jesus? Did he have a good reason to be afraid?

9. Isaiah, a prophet who lived six hundred years before Peter was born, also had a dramatic encounter with the power of God. Read Isaiah 6:1-8. Compare Isaiah's response to Peter's response. How are they similar? How did God respond to each man's fear?

10. List all the things Peter learned about Jesus in this passage:

## MAKE IT REAL

Peter learned significant things about Jesus' true identity in Luke 5, yet there was still much he did not know. Fortunately, we know the rest of the story. Jesus possesses divine power and knowledge because He is the only Son of God, fully human and fully divine. And He can forgive Peter's sins and our sins because He willingly died on the cross as a perfect sacrifice for our sins. He then rose from the dead, conquering sin and death. Now He offers forgiveness to everyone who will accept it—to everyone who, like Peter, will acknowledge their sin and will turn to Jesus for eternal life.

Have you believed (become persuaded) that Jesus truly is the Son of God who died for your sins and rose from the dead? If not, what's holding you back? Begin by making a list here and then talk to your group or your leader about your objections. If you already believe, write out the objections you hear most often from others, and discuss with your group or leader some ways you might address them.

11. Reflect on the following passages about the power and glory of Jesus. Read each passage and note some of the key words below. Then spend a few minutes praising Jesus for how awesome He is and thanking Him for choosing to love sinners like us.

- John 1:1-5

- Colossians 1:13-20

- Hebrews 1:1-4

## MEMORIZE

For this week, memorize 1 John 5:13:

**I write these things to you who believe in the name of the Son of God so that you may know that you have eternal life.**

If you are doing this study with a group, recite the memory verse to one another at the start of your next group discussion. Each week, add the new verse or verses to the ones you've already memorized to make sure that you remember them.

# Your Mission, Should You Choose to Accept It

Anyone who does not take his cross and follow me is not worthy of me. Whoever finds his life will lose it, and whoever loses his life for my sake will find it.

MATTHEW 10:38-39

AFTER COLLEGE, I (Blake) worked as a mechanical engineer at a small company designing electric vehicles. I spent most of my time converting a diesel bus into an electric-hybrid bus for use in Cairo, Egypt. The project proved difficult and frustrating and required a lot of unpaid overtime, so we felt a great sense of relief and satisfaction the day our team finally completed the bus and prepared it for shipment. That sense of satisfaction did not last long, however, because when the bus arrived in Egypt, authorities impounded it due to a dispute between their government and ours. Months later, it remained locked in a warehouse, collecting dust. To this day, I don't know if it ever got out!

That experience left me feeling like King Solomon must have felt as he wrote these words in the book of Ecclesiastes: "So I hated life, because the work that is done under the sun was grievous to me. All of it is meaningless, a chasing after the wind" (2:17). If I allowed my job to become my reason for living, my purpose in life, I would truly have nothing worth living for! What I needed was an eternally significant purpose, a mission or task that couldn't be sidetracked by the circumstances of this life.

That is precisely what Jesus gave Peter and the other disciples in Matthew 10: an eternally significant mission that would make a righteous and lasting impact on the world. And although that mission requires great sacrifice and effort, it promises great reward for those who embrace it. Read the following excerpts from Matthew 10:

> These are the names of the twelve apostles: first, Simon (who is called Peter) and his brother Andrew; James son of Zebedee, and his brother John; Philip and Bartholomew; Thomas and Matthew the tax collector; James son of Alphaeus, and Thaddaeus; Simon the Zealot and Judas Iscariot, who betrayed him.
>
> These twelve Jesus sent out with the following instructions: "Do not go among the Gentiles or enter any town of the Samaritans. Go rather to the lost sheep of Israel. As you go, preach this message: 'The kingdom of heaven is near.' Heal the sick, raise the dead, cleanse those who have leprosy, drive out demons. Freely you have received, freely give. . . .
>
> "I am sending you out like sheep among wolves. Therefore be as shrewd as snakes and as innocent as doves.
>
> "Be on your guard against men; they will hand you over to the local councils and flog you in their synagogues. On my account you will be brought before governors and kings as witnesses to them and to the Gentiles. But when they arrest you, do not worry about what to say or how to say it. At that time you will be given what to say, for it will not be you speaking, but the Spirit of your Father speaking through you. . . .

"Are not two sparrows sold for a penny? Yet not one of them will fall to the ground apart from the will of your Father. And even the very hairs of your head are all numbered. So don't be afraid; you are worth more than many sparrows.

"Whoever acknowledges me before men, I will also acknowledge him before my Father in heaven. But whoever disowns me before men, I will disown him before my Father in heaven. . . .

"Anyone who loves his father or mother more than me is not worthy of me; anyone who loves his son or daughter more than me is not worthy of me; and anyone who does not take his cross and follow me is not worthy of me. Whoever finds his life will lose it, and whoever loses his life for my sake will find it." (Matthew 10:2-8,16-20,29-33,37-39)

## TAKING INVENTORY

1. Complete the following sentence: I was put on earth to
   _____. Why do you believe this?

2. What does the ideal Christian life look like? In other words, if you walk faithfully with the Lord, what do you expect your life to be like?

3. What are some of the most severe trials you've faced in life? How did you respond? Fill in the following chart with your answers.

| My most severe trials in life | How I responded to each trial |
|---|---|
|  |  |
|  |  |
|  |  |
|  |  |
|  |  |
|  |  |
|  |  |
|  |  |

# WILLING TO DIE

In the two thousand years since the time of Jesus, countless men and women have suffered persecution and death as a result of their willingness to embrace Jesus' mission for their lives. One such man, Ignatius, the head elder of the church in Antioch in the late first century AD, was arrested for preaching about Jesus, taken to the Roman Colosseum, and torn apart by lions! A similar fate awaited Jim Elliot almost 1,900 years later when he was brutally killed by the Auca Indians of Ecuador while trying to reach them with the gospel.[1] Both men gave their lives for Jesus' mission. And both men did so joyfully.

As Ignatius wrote shortly before his martyrdom, "I am writing to all the Churches and I enjoin all, that I am dying willingly for God's sake, if only you do not prevent it. I beg you, do not do me an untimely kindness. Allow me to be eaten by the beasts, which are my way of reaching to God. I am God's wheat, and I am to be ground by the teeth of wild beasts, so that I may become the pure bread of Christ."[2] Ignatius welcomed the opportunity to sacrifice his life in order to show others the greatness and worth of Jesus Christ. In a similar vein, as Jim Elliot prepared to enter the mission field, he wrote in his personal journal, "He is no fool who gives what he cannot keep to gain that which he cannot lose."[3]

Both men understood that because we live in a world hostile to our faith, there will always be great risk for those who embrace Jesus' call upon their lives. In fact, as Paul promised in 2 Timothy 3:12, "Everyone who wants to live a godly life in Christ Jesus will be persecuted." Yet that suffering is, in reality, a small price to pay for the privilege of serving Jesus in an eternally significant way.

Read back over the passage in Matthew 10 as you answer the following questions. In particular, look for the reasons Jesus gives to embrace His call on your life despite the risks it involves.

## LOOK IT OVER

4. Examine Matthew 10 carefully. What key words and ideas seem particularly important in order to understand this passage? Summarize the main point of the passage in your own words.

    a. Key words:

b. Key ideas:

c. Main idea:

5. What specifically did Jesus ask His disciples to do?

>>>>>>>>>>>>>>>>>>>>>>>>>>>>>>>>>>>>>>>>>>>>>>>>>>>>>>>>>>>>>>>>>>>>>>

## ONLY TO THE JEWS?

In verses 5-6, Jesus explicitly tells His disciples to preach only to Jewish people and not to anyone else. Does God care more about Jewish people than people of every other race? No. As Genesis 3–11 records, the entire human race rebelled against God and fell into sin. So in grace God chose one man's family, the family of Abraham (later known as the nation of Israel), to become the agents of blessing and restoration to the world. But as the rest of the Old Testament reveals, this chosen family proved to be as prone to sin as the rest of the world. They couldn't save others because they couldn't even save themselves! For God's plan of worldwide restoration to begin, He first had to restore the agents of restoration, the Jews. So Jesus' ministry begins with them. Three years later, after dying and rising from the dead, Jesus extends His ministry to the entire world, telling His disciples to "go and make disciples of all nations" (Matthew 28:19).

6. Jesus knew that His disciples, Peter included, would struggle with fear. List all the promises and encouragements Jesus gave them in Matthew 10 that inspire peace and confidence.

7. According to this passage, what should a faithful follower of Jesus expect to receive from the world? How should we expect to be treated if we are faithful to Jesus?

## THINK IT THROUGH

8. What did Jesus mean by the phrase, "Freely you have received, freely give"? What had they received? What were they to give?

9. What does it mean to be "as shrewd as snakes and as innocent as doves"? What would this look like for you at school or work?

10. Based on verses 33 and 38-39, many people conclude that to have eternal life we must not only boldly proclaim the gospel to a hostile world, but we must also be willing to actually die for Jesus. While we should, indeed, be willing to die for Him, is our eternal life

at stake if we aren't willing? Why or why not? For help, turn to 1 Corinthians 3:12-15 (where "building on the foundation" is about what a person does or doesn't do in life to build God's kingdom), Ephesians 2:8-9, and Revelation 2:26-27.

## SAME MISSION, NEW MESSAGE

Jesus tells Peter and the other disciples to proclaim to the nation of Israel that "the kingdom of heaven is near." While that phrase may sound odd to us, it made perfect sense to a first-century Jew. They understood it to mean that God was about to act from heaven to re-establish His kingdom on earth through the nation of Israel. While God will one day restore the nation of Israel in fulfillment of His covenant promises in the Old Testament, He is doing something new and different today. God is drawing men and women of every race, not just Jews, into a new form of His kingdom on earth, the church. And He's doing so through faith in the sacrificial death and resurrection of Jesus. This is the good news (the literal meaning of the term "gospel" in the Bible) that we are called to proclaim to all tribes, tongues, nations, and people. Any person can enter God's kingdom this very moment simply by believing that Jesus died for his or her sins and then rose from the dead to conquer sin and death!

## MAKE IT REAL

With whom can you share the good news of the gospel this month? List three or more people in your life who don't yet know Jesus as their Savior. Begin to pray each week for opportunities to share your faith with each of them.

11. Have you suffered for your faith? When? How? If not, are you willing to?

## MEMORIZE

Review the memory verse from the previous lesson. Then memorize Matthew 28:19-20:

Therefore go and make disciples of all nations, baptizing them in the name of the Father and of the Son and of the Holy Spirit, and teaching them to obey everything I have commanded you. And surely I am with you always, to the very end of the age.

# Faith and Fear in a Fury

Immediately Jesus reached out his hand and caught him. "You of little faith," he said, "why did you doubt?"

MATTHEW 14:31

RAPPELLING OFF THE face of a cliff is one of the great rites of passage that all young people should experience. There's nothing quite like the thrill of literally taking your life in your own hands as you jump away from the edge, loosen your grip on the rope, and accelerate rapidly toward the ground. But the ride isn't fun for everyone. During college, I (Blake) supervised a rappelling station off a cliff in the Texas hill country. I treated more than a few banged-up guys and girls. Scraped knees and bloody noses were common. And surprisingly, it was often the most athletic kids who got banged up. Why? What separates the men from the boys when rappelling?

One word: faith. Those who had faith in the strength of the rope rappelled down the cliff without injury. They got to the edge and leaned back, way back, until they were nearly horizontal. With all their weight carried by the rope, they could fly safely down the cliff without harm. Their faith in the rope was rewarded with an exhilarating ride.

On the other hand, those who wouldn't trust the rope needed prompt medical attention. Rather than leaning back at the cliff edge, these guys tried to rely on their own strength and dexterity and simply walk down the cliff on their own two feet. That never works for long. As soon as the cliff face went vertical, their feet slipped out from under them and they face-planted into the rock.

Rappelling is counterintuitive. The more you rely on your strength, dexterity, and balance, the less likely you are to succeed. All that matters is faith. Will you trust the rope rather than yourself?

A similar question confronted Peter in the events of Matthew 14. In a moment of crisis, not unlike leaning over a cliff, he had to choose whether to rely on his own strength or upon the strength that Jesus provided. Read the following passage to see how Peter did in this test of faith.

Immediately Jesus made the disciples get into the boat and go on ahead of him to the other side, while he dismissed the crowd. After he had dismissed them, he went up on a mountainside by himself to pray. When evening came, he was there alone, but the boat was already a considerable distance from land, buffeted by the waves because the wind was against it.

During the fourth watch of the night Jesus went out to them, walking on the lake. When the disciples saw him walking on the lake, they were terrified. "It's a ghost," they said, and cried out in fear.

But Jesus immediately said to them: "Take courage! It is I. Don't be afraid."

"Lord, if it's you," Peter replied, "tell me to come to you on the water."

"Come," he said.

Then Peter got down out of the boat, walked on the water and came toward Jesus. But when he saw the wind, he was afraid and, beginning to sink, cried out, "Lord, save me!"

Immediately Jesus reached out his hand and caught him. "You of little faith," he said, "why did you doubt?"

And when they climbed into the boat, the wind died down. Then those who were in the boat worshiped him, saying, "Truly you are the Son of God." (verses 22-33)

## THE CHALLENGE OF FAITH

In the life of a Christian, faith is both a one-time event and an ongoing process. At a moment in time we choose to believe in the good news of the gospel—that Jesus died for our sins, rose from the dead, and now offers us eternal life as a free gift. The moment we believe, we are justified, meaning God declares us to be permanently in right standing with Him (see Romans 3:21-28). He forgives all of our sins and He sends His Holy Spirit to live within us forever (see Ephesians 1:13-14). We are, from that moment on, children of God, guaranteed to spend eternity with Him (see Romans 8:29-39).

But that does not exhaust our need for faith. Now as children of God, we are called to grow in our faith in Him. God wants us to learn to trust Him ever more fully with our lives (see Ephesians 1:15-19; Hebrews 11:1-6; 12:1-2). But as Peter's example demonstrates, that's no small task! When life becomes difficult we are tempted to trust in our own abilities and efforts to sustain us.

1. What crisis moments have you experienced in life? In those moments, did you turn to God for help, or did you rely on your own abilities, connections, or personality to sustain you?

2. Why is it so difficult for us to trust God in every area of life? Why do we so often rely on our own abilities to make our lives work?

## LOOK IT OVER

3. Examine Matthew 14 carefully. What key words and ideas seem particularly important in order to understand this passage? Summarize the main point of the passage in your own words.

a. Key words:

b. Key ideas:

c. Main idea:

4. Describe the events of this day in Jesus' life (Matthew 14:13-36 records just one day). Note that the "fourth watch of the night" means from 3 a.m. to 6 a.m.

5. How did Peter's attitude change over the course of this story? In other words, how did he feel early in the story, in the middle of the story, and at the end of the story?

>>>>>>>>>>>>>>>>>>>>>>>>>>>>>>>>>>>>>>>>>>>>>>>>>>>>>>>>>>>>>>>>

### SON OF GOD

At the end of our passage, the disciples respond to Jesus' miraculous stroll on the sea by proclaiming that He is indeed "the Son of God." When we say that about Jesus we mean that He is the second person of the Trinity: God the Son in human flesh, almighty, eternal, all-knowing, and so forth. That is what the title "Son of God" will come to mean later in the New Testament after Jesus rises from the dead. But before then, the title means something simpler. It's actually a title used in the Old Testament to refer to the king of Israel, the man whom God chose to lead His people (see Psalm 2:6-7). The prophets promised that this future king would come with miraculous power and great authority (see Isaiah 9:2-7). So when the disciples say that Jesus is the "Son of God," they mean that He is this promised king who was sent by God to rule over the nation of Israel.

## THINK IT THROUGH

6. Why did Jesus call His disciples men of "little faith"? Look in your Bible to see what miracles Jesus performed right before this event (see Matthew 14:13-21). What should the disciples have learned from these miracles?

7. What exactly should Peter and the other disciples have had greater "faith" in? In other words, what is it that they should have believed or trusted in during these events?

8. What did Peter learn about Jesus in this passage?

9. Do you think Peter's statement in verse 28 reflects wisdom or immaturity on Peter's part? Why?

10. The passage ends with the disciples worshipping Jesus. What do we learn about Jesus from the fact that He accepts their worship (see Matthew 4:8-10; Revelation 22:9)?

## REMEMBER THE FACTS

Most of the people who rappelled with me down that cliff in central Texas needed a little pep talk to get them over the edge. After all, there is nothing natural about leaning backward over a forty-foot cliff! So I reminded them of the facts. The rope they rappelled down was rated for six thousand pounds, more than enough to lift a Toyota Tundra! For extra safety, they were tied to a second rope that I controlled, a rope that passed through a safety belay that would seize up if I dropped it. And both ropes were anchored by steel bolts running deep into the granite under our feet. There was literally no way they were going to fall! The facts are just as helpful to us in our own struggle with faith. In times of crisis, we need to remember who Jesus is and what God has promised to do for us through Him.

## MAKE IT REAL

11. Look up the following passages that describe who Jesus is and what Jesus has promised to do for us. Write down the facts each passage presents that will give us confidence to trust in Him.

   • John 10:27-30


   • Romans 8:28-39


   • Philippians 4:12-13


   • Hebrews 1:1-4


   • Hebrews 4:14-16

- Hebrews 13:5-8

Which of the steps of faith listed below is God calling you to take? Beneath the appropriate statement(s), write down how you plan to take that step of faith this week. Be specific.

☐ Trust in Him to help me overcome a habitual sin

☐ Rely on Him for something I need rather than relying on myself

☐ Share my faith with somebody who doesn't know Jesus

☐ Other: _____

## MEMORIZE

Review the memory verses from the previous lessons. Then memorize Hebrews 12:1-2:

> **Therefore, since we are surrounded by such a great cloud of witnesses, let us throw off everything that hinders and the sin that so easily entangles, and let us run with perseverance the race marked out for us. Let us fix our eyes on Jesus, the author and perfecter of our faith, who for the joy set before him endured the cross, scorning its shame, and sat down at the right hand of the throne of God.**

# Two Steps Forward, Two Steps Back

"What about you?" he asked. "Who do you say I am?" Simon Peter answered, "You are the Christ, the Son of the living God."

MATTHEW 16:15-16

ON OCTOBER 25, 1964, during a game against the San Francisco 49ers, Minnesota Vikings defensive end Jim Marshall recovered a fumble by the opposing team. A highly skilled player, Marshall would eventually recover more fumbles than any other player in NFL history. Seeing an open lane, he ran the ball 66 yards into the end zone and in jubilation threw the ball into the stands.

There was only one problem: It was the wrong end zone! Marshall got turned around and ran the ball into his own team's end zone. And if that wasn't bad enough, when he threw the ball into the stands and out of bounds, he handed the 49ers a safety worth two points! Marshall didn't realize his mistake until an opposing player ran into the end zone to give him a hug. He had committed what many consider to be one of the most embarrassing mistakes in professional football history. From that game on, he was known as "Wrong Way Marshall." What began with great success turned into an epic failure.[1]

Peter experienced a similar reversal in a conversation with Jesus. He began well by demonstrating supernatural wisdom and understanding but then got "turned around" when Jesus revealed the difficulties in store for those who follow God in this hostile world. Thrown off by the idea of suffering, Peter ended up making one of the greatest blunders in the Gospels. Look at Matthew 16:13-27:

> When Jesus came to the region of Caesarea Philippi, he asked his disciples, "Who do people say the Son of Man is?"
>
> They replied, "Some say John the Baptist; others say Elijah; and still others, Jeremiah or one of the prophets."
>
> "But what about you?" he asked. "Who do you say I am?"
>
> Simon Peter answered, "You are the Christ, the Son of the living God."
>
> Jesus replied, "Blessed are you, Simon son of Jonah, for this was not revealed to you by man, but by my Father in heaven. And I tell you that you are Peter, and on this rock I will build my church, and the gates of Hades will not overcome it. I will give you the keys of the kingdom of heaven; whatever you bind on earth will be bound in heaven, and whatever you loose on earth will be loosed in heaven." Then he warned his disciples not to tell anyone that he was the Christ.
>
> From that time on Jesus began to explain to his disciples that he must go to Jerusalem and suffer many things at the hands of the elders, chief priests and teachers of the law, and that he must be killed and on the third day be raised to life.
>
> Peter took him aside and began to rebuke him. "Never, Lord!" he said. "This shall never happen to you!"
>
> Jesus turned and said to Peter, "Get behind me, Satan! You are a stumbling block to me; you do not have in mind the things of God, but the things of men."

Then Jesus said to his disciples, "If anyone would come after me, he must deny himself and take up his cross and follow me. For whoever wants to save his life will lose it, but whoever loses his life for me will find it. What good will it be for a man if he gains the whole world, yet forfeits his soul? Or what can a man give in exchange for his soul? For the Son of Man is going to come in his Father's glory with his angels, and then he will reward each person according to what he has done."

## WHAT'S IN A NAME?

By this late stage in Jesus' ministry, rumors about Him were swirling throughout Israel. His bold teaching and unprecedented miracles inspired awe and drew attention. The entire nation wondered who this man could be. Was He John the Baptist, risen from the dead, or maybe one of the great Old Testament prophets like Elijah or Jeremiah? While these rumors were certainly flattering to Jesus (these were some of the greatest men in Israel's history, after all), none of them did Him justice.

Peter understood that. He knew that Jesus was much more than just another prophet or miracle worker. Jesus was and is the "Christ." Despite what many of us assume, that's not Jesus' last name! That's His title. "Christ" is the Greek translation of the Hebrew word "Messiah," meaning "anointed one." God anointed many men in the Old Testament as kings and priests to lead His nation. Sadly, most of them dishonored God and led the nation into sin. That sin brought God's devastating punishment through the Assyrians and Babylonians, who conquered and exiled the Jews. Yet even in the midst of those tragedies, God promised to restore His people to spiritual health and physical prosperity, and to do so through one final, ultimate "Messiah." In the dark and painful centuries after the Exile, the hopes of all Jews turned to this promised anointed deliverer.

So when Peter called Jesus "Christ," it was no small thing! Peter meant that Jesus is God's promised deliverer who will restore the glory of the nation of Israel.

1. How would you answer Jesus' question in verse 15? Who do you say He is? How do you know?

2. Peter's given name was "Simon." But from Matthew 16 onward, he's referred to as "Peter," which means "the rock." How would you feel if you were in Peter's shoes and God's Son publicly renamed you "the rock"?

## LOOK IT OVER

3. Examine Matthew 16:13-27 carefully. What key words and ideas seem particularly important in order to understand this passage? Summarize the main point of the passage in your own words.

a. Key words:

b. Key ideas:

c. Main idea:

4. What names or titles are given to Jesus in this passage?

5. What did Peter do well in this passage? What did he do poorly?

»»»»»»»»»»»»»»»»»»»»»»»»»»»»»»»»»»»»»»»»»»»»»»»»»»»

## ROCK, KEY, KINGDOM

Jesus certainly gives Peter a compliment in verses 17-19. But just what is Jesus saying about Peter? Is Peter the foundation of the church? Does he have absolute authority over it? To answer that question, you need a little Greek! The name "Peter" is actually the masculine form of the Greek word *petros*, meaning "small rock." But when Jesus says "on this *rock* I will build my church," He uses the feminine form, *petras*, meaning "large rock." That doesn't refer to Peter; it refers most likely to Peter's confession in verse 16 that Jesus is "the Christ." Upon that unconquerable truth, Jesus would build His church. Furthermore, when Jesus grants Peter "the keys of the kingdom," He is not giving Peter absolute authority. Just as keys open doors, so Peter will be used by Jesus in Acts 8 and 10 to open the door of the church to both Samaritans (half-Jews) and Gentiles (everyone who's not a Jew or Samaritan).

# THINK IT THROUGH

6. Why did Peter need God the Father's help to understand that Jesus is the Christ, the Son of God (see verse 17)? Why wasn't that obvious to the Jews of Jesus' day? In other words, how did Jesus compare to what they expected their Messiah to be and to do? To help you answer this question, read the last chapter of the Old Testament, Malachi 4, which helped shape the Jews' expectations about their Messiah.

7. Why would Jesus actually command them *not* to tell others that He is the Christ (see verse 20)? Hint: Think about what happened as soon as the people in charge of the nation found out that He was the Christ (see Matthew 26:63-66). Why might Jesus have wanted to delay this event?

8. Why did Jesus call Peter "Satan" in verse 23? In what way was Peter thinking or speaking like Satan in this passage? Did he really deserve such a harsh rebuke? Why or why not?

## DRIFTING OFF CENTER

Treadmills and televisions don't always work well together, as our friend Jane learned on a particularly embarrassing day (names have been changed to protect the innocent!). She was running on a treadmill at a popular gym in front of several TVs. As luck would have it, one of her favorite shows was playing, but not on the TV directly in front of her. Instead, it was on a TV a few degrees to her right. As she got engrossed in the program, she didn't notice her feet slowly beginning to move toward the television. Inch by inch, she drifted closer to the railing on the side of the treadmill until, suddenly catching it with her right foot, she careened off balance and wiped out for everybody in the gym to see!

Something similar happened to Peter when he took his eyes away from Christ and focused instead on the world and what it offers. And it can happen to us as well. When we let ourselves get drawn into the values, possessions, and pleasures of this world, we get "off center" and, eventually, wipe out. For Peter in Matthew 16:21-23, it was the hope of fame and worldly success that tripped him up. He assumed that as a friend of God's Messiah, he would enjoy power and prosperity in this world. Because of that assumption, he was unwilling to accept God's plan for Jesus and for himself, a plan that led to suffering and persecution.

## MAKE IT REAL

Have you drifted "off center" like Peter? Are you focused on Jesus and His kingdom, or have you drifted toward the values, possessions, and pleasures of this world? To help you answer that question, list your hopes and dreams below. In other words, what things capture your attention, whether big or small, present or future? For each hope, mark whether it revolves around Jesus' values (J) or the world's (W). Note that some hopes could go either way depending on your attitude and motives toward them. So think about whether you are seeking to fulfill those hopes in order to honor Jesus or satisfy a worldly desire.

*My hopes for the future . . .*

~~~~~~~~~~~~~~~~~~~~~~~~~~~~~~~~~~~~

9. Look back over the list you created above. On an average week, what percentage of your time is focused on attaining the hopes you marked with a *W* and what percentage is focused on the hopes you marked with a *J*?

10. Like Peter, we will fail to stay focused on Christ and His kingdom if we aren't content with what God has given us in this life. Peter longed for greater fame and prosperity, and so do many of us. In what areas of your life do you struggle with contentment? That's easy to answer by completing the following question: "I would *really* be content if I could just get _____."

Your answer might be money, a possession, popularity, success in school or an organization, a date, and so on. What would you put in that blank?

11. Take a few minutes to pray for God's help in this area. If you have been living a discontented life, confess that to the Lord and ask Him to increase your contentment. If you've been spending too much time focused on attaining the things of this world, confess that to God and ask Him to give you a stronger desire for the things of His kingdom.

## MEMORIZE

Review the memory verses from the previous lessons. If you have time, recite the memory verses with a partner or with your group. Then memorize Romans 12:2:

**Do not conform any longer to the pattern of this world, but be transformed by the renewing of your mind. Then you will be able to test and approve what God's will is — his good, pleasing and perfect will.**

# The Last Are First

> Whoever exalts himself will be humbled, and whoever humbles himself will be exalted.
>
> MATTHEW 23:12

IN PREPARATION FOR World War II, the Nazis designed and built the Gustav cannon, the largest artillery piece ever used in warfare. Four stories tall, twenty feet wide, and weighing in at 1,344 tons, the behemoth could fire a 15,600-pound shell and hit a target over twenty-three miles away! The shell carried enough force to pierce through twenty-three feet of reinforced concrete.[1] No fortification in the world could stand for long against a weapon like that.

But it didn't matter. The massive gun and its twin, the Dora, saw very little action. In fact, they fired a grand total of forty-eight shells in combat during the entire war! Their designers had failed to realize that a new era had dawned in warfare. Massive, fixed fortifications had been replaced by fast, mechanized battalions that could rapidly outflank the enemy. In that new era of warfare, the Gustav's massive size was not merely irrelevant, it was a liability. The gun took a crew of 250 men fifty-four hours to assemble (not including the additional crew of 2,500 men required to lay the specialized railroad track on which the gun sat!). By the time they were finished, the battle had moved on. As a result, their massive cannon, which would have been the envy of every army in the previous era, was worse than useless.

Jesus' disciples struggled in a similar manner. He proclaimed the dawn of a new era on earth called "the kingdom of God." When this kingdom comes, there will be a great reversal of values. What is valuable in this present world will no longer be valuable then, and what is of little value now will be of great value then. But Jesus' disciples struggled to make that transition, as the two passages below demonstrate:

> They came to Capernaum. When he was safe at home, he asked them, "What were you discussing on the road?"
>
> The silence was deafening—they had been arguing with one another over who among them was greatest.
>
> He sat down and summoned the Twelve. "So you want first place? Then take the last place. Be the servant of all."
>
> He put a child in the middle of the room. Then, cradling the little one in his arms, he said, "Whoever embraces one of these children as I do embraces me, and far more than me—God who sent me." (Mark 9:33-37, MSG)

This conversation occurred midway through Jesus' ministry. Sadly, despite Jesus' clear teaching on the subject, His disciples failed to learn the lesson. Some time later, during the Last Supper, they made the same mistake.

> Also a dispute arose among them as to which of them was considered to be greatest. Jesus said to them, "The kings of the Gentiles lord it over them; and those who exercise authority over them call themselves Benefactors. But you are not to be like that. Instead, the greatest among you should be like the youngest, and the one who rules like the one who serves. For who is greater, the one who is at the table or the one who serves? Is it not the one who is at the table? But I am among you as one who serves. (Luke 22:24-27)

## GREATNESS THROUGH HUMILITY

Do you see the radical reversal of values that Jesus proclaimed in these passages? In the midst of a world that rewards pride, arrogance, and self-promotion, Jesus praised humility, selflessness, and service. True greatness in the new era of God's kingdom belongs to those who choose the path of humility, who sacrifice their rights, desires, and reputations to serve others. Jesus did not merely teach the value of humility; He modeled it in both His life and death. As Philippians 2:5-8 says,

> Your attitude should be the same as that of Christ Jesus: Who, being in very nature God, did not consider equality with God something to be grasped, but made himself nothing, taking the very nature of a servant, being made in human likeness. And being found in appearance as a man, he humbled himself and became obedient to death—even death on a cross!

Jesus gave His life as a sacrifice for us. That is and will always be the ultimate expression of humility.

1. Just as in Peter's day, our culture often rewards pride and self-promotion. Can you think of recent examples at your job, in school, in your community, or in your culture (especially TV and movies) where pride and self-promotion were praised or rewarded?

2. Why is it often difficult for us to be humble like Jesus?

## LOOK IT OVER

3. Examine Mark 9:33-37 and Luke 22:24-27 carefully. What key words and ideas seem particularly important in order to understand these passages? Summarize the main point of the passages in your own words.

  a. Key words:

  b. Key ideas:

  c. Main idea:

4. It's ironic that the disciples expressed their pride and ambition right after Jesus' words in Mark 9:30-32. Look up these verses. What was Jesus saying? How should the disciples have responded to His statement?

5. Jesus wanted His disciples to pursue "greatness," but not as they had defined the word. In the space below, list all of the descriptions Jesus gave in Mark 9:33-37 and Luke 22:24-27 for what true greatness looks like.

## THINK IT THROUGH

6. What did Jesus mean when He said, "If anyone wants to be first, he must be the very last" (Mark 9:35)? What exactly was He telling His disciples to do? For a helpful illustration from Jesus, see Luke 14:7-11.

»»»»»»»»»»»»»»»»»»»»»»»»»»»»»»»»»»»»»»»»»»»»»»»»»»»»»»»»

## CHILDREN IN THE ANCIENT WORLD

Children were thought of very differently in Jesus' day than in our own day. While we will stop anything to admire, praise, and protect a child, first-century Jewish and Greco-Roman society tended to ignore children. Greek society, in particular, celebrated intelligence, strength, and self-control—all things a child lacks. Therefore, children were regarded as the least significant members of the community and of the family.[2] A child was often put under the authority of a slave until he or she reached adulthood. In fact, the word for "child" in Aramaic (the primary language Jesus spoke), was the same word used for "servant"![3]

7. In Mark 9, how do verses 36-37 relate to verse 35? In other words, why did Jesus turn His attention to a child after challenging His disciples about pride? Why did He associate embracing (literally: "welcoming") a child with welcoming God?

8. In Luke 22:27, Jesus mentioned His example of service toward others. In what ways did Jesus serve His disciples and others (for two examples, see John 13:5-15 and 1 Peter 2:21-24)?

»»»»»»»»»»»»»»»»»»»»»»»»»»»»»»»»»»»»»»»»»»»»»»»»»»»»»»»

## BENEFACTORS: CELEBRITIES OF THE ANCIENT WORLD

In Jesus' day, a "benefactor" or "helper of the people" was a common title for kings and an honorary title bestowed on other prominent people for some great achievement or public service.[4] Those who possessed the title didn't perform public service out of love or humility but out of selfish ambition to gain this celebrity title. By the very nature of the title, these acts of "service" had to be highly public — you had to show off your "service" for all to see! It worked much like today's celebrity culture that rewards those who praise and promote themselves. And in that sense, it was the opposite of the humble and inconspicuous attitude that Christ modeled and taught to His disciples.[5]

## HUMILITY IN A ME-FIRST WORLD

We live in a world that rewards self-promotion. Reality TV stars earn millions of dollars by capturing our attention with their outrageous behavior (the Kardashian clan earned an astounding $65 million in 2011).[6] Websites quantify our popularity by counting our "friends" and "followers." Colleges and companies choose one of us over another based on our ability to sell ourselves and our accomplishments. Success often depends on our ability to promote ourselves above others.

That's why humility will be a difficult and costly road for us to walk. It may cost us socially because humility is, by definition, not the best way to attract people's attention! It may cost us professionally because humility is not viewed as a virtue by most companies.

But while humility will cost us now, it will benefit us later. When Jesus comes again to establish His kingdom, He will exalt the humble and humble the exalted. Those who live humbly and sacrificially in this life, as He did, will share in His rule over the nations in the next life (see Psalm 37:10-11; Matthew 5:3,5; 19:27-30).

# MAKE IT REAL

Complete the following exercise to assess how you are doing in each of the three arenas of life listed. For each arena, start by listing an example or two of a specific time in the last few months when you spoke or acted in a prideful way (chose to put your rights, desires, or reputation first at the expense of someone else's good). Next, list one or two specific, concrete choices you can make this week to put humility into practice in each arena (practical steps you'll take to place the good of others above your desires, rights, and reputation).

**At home:**

- A time I recently acted in pride or selfishness:


- Concrete steps I'll take to serve others:


**Among friends:**

- A time I recently acted in pride or selfishness:


- Concrete steps I'll take to serve others:

**At work or school:**

- A time I recently acted in pride or selfishness:

- Concrete steps I'll take to serve others:

9. True greatness includes caring about those whom society regards as "least." Is there a person in your circle of friends, acquaintances, coworkers, or classmates who often gets ignored or ridiculed by others? What specifically can you do in the next few weeks to show God's love to this person?

What could you do this month as a group to show God's sacrificial love to an individual, family, or group that has typically been neglected by our success-driven society (for example, those who are poor, homeless, sick, elderly, disabled, different)? Once you've chosen, take the time to plan the details. Use the following list to help you plan. You might even wish to assign group members to certain tasks.

Whom we will serve:

Our purpose for serving:

Date(s):

Person to contact to get involved:

List of others we'll need to include:

Other details:

~~~~~~~~~~~~~~~~~~~~~~~~~~~~~~~~~~~~~~~~

## MEMORIZE

Review the memory verse from the previous lesson. Then memorize Philippians 2:3-4:

**Do nothing out of selfish ambition or vain conceit, but in humility consider others better than yourselves. Each of you should look not only to your own interests, but also to the interests of others.**

# Epic Fail

Pride goes before destruction, a haughty spirit before a fall.

PROVERBS 16:18

"PRIDE GOES BEFORE a fall." I (Blake) suffered the truth of that proverb on a beautiful autumn day near the end of my college career. I was enjoying my favorite class: mountain biking. (Awesome electives are just one of the countless advantages of attending a large university!) This particular day carried special significance because, after many months of saving every penny, I had just purchased a high-end bike outfitted with the very best components, lightest frame, and most supple shock absorber reasonable money could buy. The bike proved as fast as it was beautiful. Even our teacher gawked over it. In fact, she was so impressed, she asked me to lead the class on the trail that day. I felt on top of the world, respected by the guys in the class and, I hoped, at least a little more attractive to the girls.

But my pride came crashing down (literally!) at the first creek crossing. A ten-foot drop ended in a tight gully. I flew down the drop but did not yet realize just how supple my front suspension was. It instantly absorbed the bike's momentum, but not my own. I went over the handlebars headfirst into the opposite bank. Because my feet were still firmly clipped into my pedals, this left me bottom up with my new bike very uncomfortably on top of me. Worst of all, the entire class, still perched at the top of the crossing, saw it all. I slowly extracted myself from my bike while the class flew by, and then gingerly rode back to my car with my body aching from the impact.

Moments like that remind me that I am not nearly as strong, graceful, or intelligent as I am tempted to believe I am. In reality, we are all weak, fallible, and in desperate need of God's strength and power. Without Him, we can accomplish nothing of genuine, lasting value. As Jesus put it in John 15:5, "I am the vine, you are the branches; he who abides in Me and I in him, he bears much fruit, for apart from Me you can do nothing" (NASB).

Just as we so often do, Peter resisted that truth. He saw himself as Jesus' right-hand man—a faithful friend and fellow soldier ready to help his King usher in the coming kingdom! Peter radiated confidence and boldness when in the presence of His Lord, as the following passage demonstrates:

> "Simon, Simon, Satan has asked to sift you as wheat. But I have prayed for you, Simon, that your faith may not fail. And when you have turned back, strengthen your brothers."
>
> But he replied, "Lord, I am ready to go with you to prison and to death."
>
> Jesus answered, "I tell you, Peter, before the rooster crows today, you will deny three times that you know me." (Luke 22:31-34)

Peter strongly resisted Jesus' prophetic words. Displaying the rashness that had proven so common during Peter's early years, he promised to suffer and die with Jesus. A few hours later, Peter did indeed act with courage and boldness to defend his Lord, as the following passage recounts:

So Judas led the way to the garden, and the Roman soldiers and police sent by the high priests and Pharisees followed. They arrived there with lanterns and torches and swords. . . .

Just then Simon Peter, who was carrying a sword, pulled it from its sheath and struck the Chief Priest's servant, cutting off his right ear. Malchus was the servant's name.

Jesus ordered Peter, "Put back your sword. Do you think for a minute I'm not going to drink this cup the Father gave me?" (John 18:3,10-11, MSG)

Peter was ready to fight for Jesus, but was he ready to suffer for Him? Though Jesus could have called down twelve legions of angels (72,000! see Matthew 26:53), He willingly submitted to His Father's plan and surrendered to the soldiers. With their Master now bound and seemingly defeated, the disciples faced a grueling choice. Would they cut their losses and save themselves, or would they stay loyal to Him when it meant suffering and apparent defeat?

Arresting Jesus, they marched him off and took him into the house of the Chief Priest. Peter followed, but at a safe distance. In the middle of the courtyard some people had started a fire and were sitting around it, trying to keep warm. One of the serving maids sitting at the fire noticed him, then took a second look and said, "This man was with him!"

He denied it, "Woman, I don't even know him."

A short time later, someone else noticed him and said, "You're one of them."

But Peter denied it: "Man, I am not."

About an hour later, someone else spoke up, really ada-mant: "He's got to have been with him! He's got 'Galilean' written all over him."

Peter said, "Man, I don't know what you're talking about." At that very moment, the last word hardly off his lips, a rooster crowed. Just then, the Master turned and looked at Peter. Peter remembered what the Master had said to him: "Before the rooster crows, you will deny me three times." He went out and cried and cried and cried. (Luke 22:54-62, MSG)

1. Think of a challenging time when you felt bold and acted courageously, as Peter did early in this story. Why did you feel that way? What happened?

2. Think of a challenging time when you felt scared and acted cowardly, as Peter did at the end of the story. Why did you feel that way? What happened?

## LOOK IT OVER

3. Examine the passages above carefully. What key words and ideas seem particularly important in order to understand these events? Summarize the main point of these passages in your own words.

   a. Key words:

b. Key ideas:

c. Main idea:

4. What did Peter do well in these passages? What did he do poorly?

5. Describe the changes in Peter's attitudes and emotions during the events recorded in these passages. What was his attitude/emotion . . .

- In the first passage?

- During Jesus' arrest?

- Around the campfire?

- At the end of the story?

# THINK IT THROUGH

6. What do you learn about Satan in the first passage? How does he relate to God? How does he treat God's people?

7. Based on the context, what does it mean for faith to "fail" (Luke 22:32)? Would such a failure have cost Peter his eternal relationship with God (see Romans 8:35-39)? Why or why not? Where does the strength of your faith fit into Paul's list in these verses?

8. Why didn't Jesus fight back? He certainly had the capacity to do so. After all, He's God and could have instantaneously wiped out His enemies. So why didn't He? In other words, why did God the Father's "cup" for Jesus (John 18:11) include surrender (see Isaiah 53:1-12)?

9. Why did Peter's boldness toward the soldiers melt into cowardice when questioned by a few servants?

## GOOD NEWS IN THE MIDST OF FAILURE

As Peter ran weeping from the campfire, overwhelmed by shame and guilt, little did he realize that on the following day (Good Friday) Jesus would die for the very betrayal Peter had just committed. Jesus' death paid the debt of all human sin. From the first sin of Adam to the last sin humans will commit, all of our sin was placed upon Jesus on the cross. He suffered God's punishment, which our sin deserved, so that we could be declared righteous and be forgiven by God. On the basis of Jesus' propitiatory death (a succinct way of saying that Jesus' sacrifice satisfied the righteous wrath of God), God offers forgiveness and eternal life as a free gift to everyone who accepts it in faith.

What good news for all of us who, like Peter, have failed to be faithful to Jesus! If we've trusted in Him as our Savior, then no matter how often we betray Him through our sinful thoughts, words, and actions, His grace forgives us and keeps us safe in the love of God (see Romans 8:38-39). As Paul said in Romans 5:20, "Where sin increased, grace increased all the more"!

## MAKE IT REAL

10. How does God want you to respond when you sin (see 1 John 1:8-9)?


- What does it mean to "confess"?


- Are there specific sins you need to confess to God? What's keeping you from doing so?

Peter's sin resulted, at least in part, from his failure to recognize his vulnerabilities. If we can identify ahead of time the specific temptations and situations that prime us for sin, we can often avoid failure by either avoiding those circumstances or by seeking help from God and other believers. Identify your vulnerabilities below.

- What sins tempt you and trip you up the most?

- What circumstances increase your susceptibility to sin (for example, sleep deprivation, busyness, late nights, too much free time)?

- What emotions and attitudes heighten your temptations?

- What people or groups of people tempt you toward sin?

Looking at the lists you created above, what steps can you take to reduce your temptations and grow in victory over sin?

11. Spend a few minutes in prayer thanking God for sending His Son
    to die for your sins and confessing any known sin to the Lord.

## MEMORIZE

Review the memory verses from the previous lesson. Challenge yourself
to recite all of the verses from the first five lessons with a partner. Then
memorize Romans 8:1-2:

> **Therefore, there is now no condemnation for those who
> are in Christ Jesus, because through Christ Jesus the
> law of the Spirit of life set me free from the law of sin
> and death.**

# Gracious Save

Jesus said to Simon Peter, "Simon, son of John, do you love me more than these?"

"Yes, Master, you know I love you."

Jesus said, "Feed my lambs."

JOHN 21:15, MSG

TRAITORS LED A captured warrior, tightly bound with ropes, toward an army of his enemies. They shouted in triumph as he approached. Their long string of humiliations at his hands was finally going to be avenged. But as they gathered around their prey, something unexpected happened. Supernatural power flooded into his body. He snapped the ropes like thread and reached for the only weapon available: a dead donkey's jawbone lying near his feet. Though he faced thousands of well-armed soldiers, his rage couldn't be stopped. He slaughtered a thousand men before his enemies could flee.

Though fit for a Hollywood blockbuster, this is actually a biblical story, the story of Samson as told in Judges 15. On that bloody day, God's Spirit enabled Samson to defeat the Philistine army that had oppressed the Israelites for forty years.

But Samson had a fatal weakness: lust. After years of getting away with it, he finally saw his sin catch up to him. Blinded by his lust for a Philistine woman named Delilah, Samson foolishly revealed to her the secret of his amazing strength: God's power would be withdrawn if his hair was cut. Out of loyalty to her people, Delilah had his hair cut while he slept. Samson awoke surrounded by soldiers he could no longer overcome. They gouged out his eyes, bound him in shackles, and threw him in prison. Samson's failure was epic. Because of his sin, Israel's greatest hero was reduced to a weak, blind prisoner. He had sacrificed his own freedom and the freedom of his nation. Imagine the guilt and shame that must have overwhelmed Samson in prison.

Peter felt that same painful guilt after he denied Jesus. When we concluded lesson 6, Peter was running from the campfire, weeping bitterly from shame and regret. Like Samson, Peter probably assumed that his heroic service to God had ended—just another tragic example of a great man ruined by sin. He was finished.

Or was he? Read the passage below to see how Jesus responded to Peter after his epic failure:

> After this, Jesus appeared again to the disciples, this time at the Tiberias Sea (the Sea of Galilee). This is how he did it: Simon Peter, Thomas (nicknamed "Twin"), Nathanael from Cana in Galilee, the brothers Zebedee, and two other disciples were together. Simon Peter announced, "I'm going fishing."
>
> The rest of them replied, "We're going with you." They went out and got in the boat. They caught nothing that night. When the sun came up, Jesus was standing on the beach, but they didn't recognize him.
>
> Jesus spoke to them: "Good morning! Did you catch anything for breakfast?"
>
> They answered, "No."
>
> He said, "Throw the net off the right side of the boat and see what happens."

They did what he said. All of a sudden there were so many fish in it, they weren't strong enough to pull it in.

Then the disciple Jesus loved said to Peter, "It's the Master!"

When Simon Peter realized that it was the Master, he threw on some clothes, for he was stripped for work, and dove into the sea. The other disciples came in by boat for they weren't far from land, a hundred yards or so, pulling along the net full of fish. When they got out of the boat, they saw a fire laid, with fish and bread cooking on it.

Jesus said, "Bring some of the fish you've just caught." Simon Peter joined them and pulled the net to shore—153 big fish! And even with all those fish, the net didn't rip.

Jesus said, "Breakfast is ready." Not one of the disciples dared ask, "Who are you?" They knew it was the Master.

Jesus then took the bread and gave it to them. He did the same with the fish. This was now the third time Jesus had shown himself alive to the disciples since being raised from the dead.

After breakfast, Jesus said to Simon Peter, "Simon, son of John, do you love me more than these?"

"Yes, Master, you know I love you."

Jesus said, "Feed my lambs."

He then asked a second time, "Simon, son of John, do you love me?"

"Yes, Master, you know I love you."

Jesus said, "Shepherd my sheep."

Then he said it a third time: "Simon, son of John, do you love me?"

Peter was upset that he asked for the third time, "Do you love me?" so he answered, "Master, you know everything there is to know. You've got to know that I love you."

Jesus said, "Feed my sheep. I'm telling you the very truth now: When you were young you dressed yourself and went wherever you wished, but when you get old you'll have to stretch out your hands while someone else dresses you and takes you where you don't want to go." He said this to hint at the kind of death by which Peter would glorify God. And then he commanded, "Follow me." (John 21:1-19, MSG)

## A LEADER RESTORED

Let's return for a moment to the sad story of Samson. As he languished in prison, his hair began to grow back. One evening the Philistine lords threw an enormous party to celebrate their victory over Samson. They brought him up from the dungeon to serve as live entertainment for the thousands of Philistines who packed the palace that night. To ensure that everybody had a good view, Samson was placed at the center of the building, between the twin support columns. That was a fatal mistake because as Samson's hair had returned, so had his supernatural strength. He pleaded with God to give him one last victory over the Philistines. And then, filled with superhuman power, he knocked over the columns, causing the palace roof to collapse. Samson sacrificed himself to kill three thousand of Israel's enemies. In the end, he killed more Philistines after his epic failure than he did in all the years before it!

Like Samson, Peter also deserved to be kicked off of God's team — both of them had failed miserably. But God doesn't give us what we deserve. God not only kept Samson and Peter on His team, He even restored them to positions of leadership. He used them to accomplish amazing things even after their failures. In fact, in both cases, the men accomplished more for God's kingdom after their failures than they did before! That's the very definition of grace: God gives us good that we don't deserve.

1. How would you expect Jesus to treat Peter after he deserted Him in His hour of greatest need?

2. How do you think God responds to you when you fail Him? How does He feel about you? How does He feel about your sin?

3. Do you feel qualified to be a leader in your church? Why or why not?

## LOOK IT OVER

4. Examine John 21 carefully. What key words and ideas seem particularly important in order to understand this passage? Summarize the main point of the passage in your own words.

   a. Key words:

   b. Key ideas:

c.  Main idea:

5. List all the parallels you see between the events of this chapter and events from the passages that you've studied in previous lessons.

6. Describe how Peter reacted to seeing Jesus in chapter 21. How did Peter feel toward Jesus?

## THINK IT THROUGH

7. Peter had committed what many consider to be the greatest sin of all: public apostasy (he publicly denied his allegiance to Jesus). Yet Jesus forgave Peter. Biblically speaking, what does it mean for God to forgive us? What does His forgiveness of our sins look like (see Psalm 103:10-12; Isaiah 43:25; Colossians 2:13-14)?

8. Jesus restored Peter to leadership. But is it always appropriate to restore to leadership an elder, deacon, or pastor who commits a serious public sin (see 1 Timothy 3:1-2,7-11)? Why or why not?

## WELCOME TO THE FOLD: WHAT IT MEANS TO BE A SHEEP

Have you ever wondered why, throughout the Old and New Testaments, God refers to His people as "sheep"? That's not exactly a compliment. Though sheep were valuable in the ancient world (wealth was often measured in the number of sheep you owned!), they were also among the least intelligent and weakest members of the animal kingdom. Because they were small and lacked horns, the sheep of ancient Israel were defenseless. They were easy prey for lions, bears, hyenas, foxes, and even large birds! They also lacked common sense. Sheep wouldn't hesitate to drink from stagnant, polluted puddles or to eat poisonous plants. They suffered from herd mentality. If one sheep wandered into a dangerous ravine, the rest would follow to their death. They couldn't even forage for themselves. Without a shepherd, the sheep would starve.

So why does God call us "sheep"? Because it reminds us that in every way we are utterly dependent upon Him. Though we pride ourselves on our strength, intelligence, and independence, we would perish without God's help just as a sheep would perish without a shepherd. Fortunately, God graciously offers to be our Good Shepherd, taking care of our every need in this life and in the next.

9. What does it mean to "shepherd" or "tend" Jesus' sheep? What exactly did Jesus want Peter to do (see Acts 20:28-31; 1 Peter 5:1-3)?

10. According to the verses below, what does it mean to love the Lord? In other words, how is love described in each passage?

- Matthew 22:35-40

- John 14:15; 15:9-14

- 1 John 2:15-16

- 1 John 4:18-21

## RESURRECTION

The course of human history changed radically between Peter's failure and restoration. While Peter hid in shame, Jesus carried His cross to Golgotha to die as a sacrifice for our sins. As we discussed in lesson 6, Jesus' death provided propitiation—His sacrifice satisfied God's righteous wrath against our sin and provided a way for God to forgive us. That's why we focus on Jesus' death when we share the gospel with other people.

But we must not forget that the cross is only half the story! If Jesus' ministry had ended at the cross, then sin, death, and Satan would have won. The Son of God would have been defeated. And, as Paul concluded in 1 Corinthians 15:17, "If Christ has not been raised, your faith is futile; you are still in your sins." Without the Resurrection, we have no hope.

But Jesus *was* raised from the dead. And by resurrecting His Son, God has given us hope. He overcame sin, death, and Satan once and for all so that we have nothing to fear. That's why Peter could have hope even after such an epic failure. If God's powerful love could overcome

death, then it could overcome anything in Peter's life, just as it can overcome anything in ours. Because of the Resurrection, there is always a
new day and a new opportunity for us to serve God! As Paul said in
Romans 6:4, "Just as Christ was raised from the dead by the glory of the
Father, we too might walk in newness of life" (ESV).

## MAKE IT REAL

11. Do you believe that God has forgiven you in the biblical sense:
forever removing all of your sin? Why or why not?

• What passages would you use to defend your answer?

Just like Peter, all believers are called to serve and lead in some way
among God's people, the church. Complete the exercise below to
assess where you are in your leadership.

Check only one of the following and complete the attached sentence(s).

☐ I'm not really interested in being a leader in the church because . . .

☐ I'd like to be a leader in the church, but am not yet ready because . . .

☐ I'm ready, but don't know where to serve. (If this is you, answer the following to help identify an ideal place to serve.)

• My primary skills, talents, and abilities are . . .


• The ministries and activities of the church that I feel drawn to (for example, music, youth ministry, world missions) are . . .


• The amount of time each week I can give is . . .


☐ I'm already a leader in the church! I serve in the following ministry or ministries . . .

---

12. Looking back over what you learned from question 10, can you honestly say that you love the Lord? Why or why not? What steps do you need to take this week to grow in your love for Him?

## MEMORIZE

Review the memory verses from the previous lesson. Then memorize Psalm 103:10-12:

> **He does not treat us as our sins deserve or repay us according to our iniquities. For as high as the heavens are above the earth, so great is his love for those who fear him; as far as the east is from the west, so far has he removed our transgressions from us.**

# A New Man

You will receive power when the Holy Spirit comes on you;
and you will be my witnesses in Jerusalem, and in all Judea
and Samaria, and to the ends of the earth.

ACTS 1:8

IN JUNE 2000, sixty-three-year-old Peter Houghton prepared for death. His long battle with cardiomyopathy, a severe disease of the heart muscle, was coming to an end. He was too weak to qualify for a heart transplant, so he made his peace with death. But then his doctors offered him one last option: he could volunteer to be the first test patient for a new heart-assist device called the Jarvis 2000. He gladly accepted the offer; after all, what did he have to lose? After an eight-hour surgery, Houghton awoke with a state-of-the-art titanium turbine, about the size of a C-battery, embedded in his dysfunctional heart.

He had made a wise choice. With the tiny heart pump providing constant blood circulation to his body, he quickly regained his strength. Over the next few years he participated in a ninety-one-mile charity walk, wrote a book, lectured all around the world, and hiked the Swiss Alps. Because of this new source of power beating in his chest, he was quite literally a new man![1]

The apostle Peter experienced an even more miraculous transformation shortly after Jesus rose from the dead and ascended into heaven. Our once brash fisherman—prone to arrogance when circumstances were good and cowardice when they weren't—became a radically new man when the Spirit of God entered into Him during the Jewish feast of Pentecost.

When the day of Pentecost came, they were all together in one place. Suddenly a sound like the blowing of a violent wind came from heaven and filled the whole house where they were sitting. They saw what seemed to be tongues of fire that separated and came to rest on each of them. All of them were filled with the Holy Spirit and began to speak in other tongues as the Spirit enabled them.

Now there were staying in Jerusalem God-fearing Jews from every nation under heaven. When they heard this sound, a crowd came together in bewilderment, because each one heard them speaking in his own language. (Acts 2:1-6)

Once again Peter faced a test of courage as he stood before the same crowd who had crucified Jesus just a few weeks before. But this time, instead of fleeing in fear, Peter stood up and spoke boldly through the power of the Holy Spirit.

"Men of Israel, listen to this: Jesus of Nazareth was a man accredited by God to you by miracles, wonders and signs, which God did among you through him, as you yourselves know. This man was handed over to you by God's set purpose and foreknowledge; and you, with the help of wicked men, put him to death by nailing him to the cross. But God raised him from the dead, freeing him from the agony of death, because it was impossible for death to keep its hold on him. . . .

"God has raised this Jesus to life, and we are all witnesses of the fact. Exalted to the right hand of God, he has received from the Father the promised Holy Spirit and has poured out what you now see and hear. For David did not ascend to heaven, and yet he said,

"'The Lord said to my Lord:
"Sit at my right hand
until I make your enemies
a footstool for your feet.'"

"Therefore let all Israel be assured of this: God has made this Jesus, whom you crucified, both Lord and Christ."

When the people heard this, they were cut to the heart and said to Peter and the other apostles, "Brothers, what shall we do?"

Peter replied, "Repent and be baptized, every one of you, in the name of Jesus Christ for the forgiveness of your sins. And you will receive the gift of the Holy Spirit. . . .

Those who accepted his message were baptized, and about three thousand were added to their number that day. (Acts 2:22-24,32-38,41)

Empowered by the Holy Spirit, Peter courageously proclaimed Christ. God used his testimony to draw thousands of Jews to salvation that day. Peter exhibited that same boldness a short time later when, after miraculously healing a crippled man, he and John were arrested and brought before the Sanhedrin, the religious leadership of Israel.

Then Peter, filled with the Holy Spirit, said to them: "Rulers and elders of the people! If we are being called to account today for an act of kindness shown to a cripple and are asked how he was healed, then know this, you and all the people of Israel: It is by the name of Jesus Christ of Nazareth, whom you crucified but whom God raised from the dead, that this man stands before you healed. He is

> "'the stone you builders rejected,
> which has become the capstone.'

Salvation is found in no one else, for there is no other name under heaven given to men by which we must be saved."

When they saw the courage of Peter and John and realized that they were unschooled, ordinary men, they were astonished and they took note that these men had been with Jesus. . . .

Then they called them in again and commanded them not to speak or teach at all in the name of Jesus. But Peter and John replied, "Judge for yourselves whether it is right in God's sight to obey you rather than God. For we cannot help speaking about what we have seen and heard." (Acts 4:8-13,18-20)

## UNEXPECTED BRAVERY

It's hard to believe that this is the same man who had cowered before servants just a few weeks earlier! Now he fearlessly testified before thousands of people and courageously defied the most powerful group of spiritual leaders in the nation. Peter's radical transformation demonstrates the power that is available to God's people through God's Spirit. Ever since the day of Pentecost, those who trust Jesus for eternal life receive the gift of the Holy Spirit. The Spirit lives permanently within believers, filling us with strength to overcome sin (see Romans 8:2-4; Galatians 5:16), giving us spiritual gifts and abilities for service (see 1 Peter 4:10-11), and producing in us the "fruit of the Spirit" (Galatians 5:22-23: love, joy, peace, patience, kindness, goodness, faithfulness, gentleness, self-control).

1. Compare your life as a Christian to your life before you trusted in Jesus. Do you see evidence of God's Spirit at work in and through you? If you have not yet chosen to trust in Jesus, are there areas of your life you would like to see change? What are they? Do you think Jesus could make those changes? Why or why not?

2. If God gave you an opportunity like He gave Peter, to boldly preach the gospel to thousands of people, would you be ready? Why or why not?

   • If not, would you be ready to proclaim the gospel in front of an audience of just a few people?

## LOOK IT OVER

3. Examine the passages from Acts carefully. What key words and ideas seem particularly important in order to understand these events? Summarize the main point of the passages in your own words.

   a. Key words:

b. Key ideas:

c. Main idea of Acts 2:

d. Main idea of Acts 4:8-13,18-20:

4. List all of the truths that Peter taught about Jesus in these passages.

5. Looking over all the included passages, summarize the message that Peter preached. What exactly was he saying to the crowds and to the Sanhedrin?

»»»»»»»»»»»»»»»»»»»»»»»»»»»»»»»»»»»»»»»»»»»»»»»»»»»»»

## "REPENT AND BE BAPTIZED"

When the crowd of Jews in Acts 2 desperately asked Peter, "What shall we do?" he told them to repent and be baptized. What exactly did Peter mean by these commands and how do they relate to faith, the sole requirement for salvation according to the gospel?

First, "repent" simply means "to turn from one thing to its opposite." In Acts 2, Peter spoke to Jewish men and women who had publicly rejected and crucified Jesus a few weeks prior. As a result, they were in danger of experiencing God's imminent punishment upon the nation of Israel (see Luke 19:41-44). To escape that fate, they needed to "repent" of that rejection by doing the opposite: publicly identifying and aligning themselves with Jesus.

Second, having repented of their rejection of Jesus, they were to be baptized in water. It may seem as if Peter was adding a work, baptism, to faith as a requirement of salvation. But that's not the case. In Peter's day, water baptism was what everyone did immediately *after* believing the gospel (see Acts 8:35-38 and 10:42-48, which prove that salvation comes *before* water baptism). Baptism was simply the way to publicly demonstrate the inner reality of their new faith in Christ and their identification with Him. Much like wedding rings act as a symbol of marriage today, baptism was the visible symbol Peter used to show the invisible reality of faith.

# THINK IT THROUGH

6. While the Holy Spirit provides all the strength we need to walk in holiness and serve God, we still must choose to tap into His strength. In other words, we have a part to play in living this new, transformed life. Look up each of the following passages and write down our part in this process of transformation.

   • Romans 12:1-2

- Galatians 5:16-18 (think particularly about what the phrase "walk by the Spirit" [ESV] means in verse 16)

- Ephesians 5:18 (think about the connection between getting drunk and being filled with the Spirit)

- Philippians 2:12-13

7. In both Acts 2 and Acts 4, amazing, public miracles occurred immediately before Peter preached. What was the purpose for these miracles? In other words, why would God do these miracles right before Peter took the stage?

8. When Jesus chose Peter as an apostle, He chose an ordinary, middle-class, relatively uneducated man. When that ordinary man became an extraordinary witness for Christ, what was the result (see Acts 4:13; 2 Corinthians 4:7; 12:9-10)?

# FROM SLAVE TRADER TO SAINT

Peter is just one of countless men and women transformed by God's Spirit. John Newton, born in England in 1725, was another. A sailor on several merchant and military ships, Newton developed a reputation for insubordination and vulgarity. On one occasion, he received a dozen lashes for trying to desert his ship. On another, he was thrown into the brig for writing obscene songs about his captain and teaching them to the entire crew. Later, aboard the ship *Greyhound*, he became known as one of the most profane men the captain had ever met—quite a feat for someone who lived among sailors universally known for their profanity! Worst of all, Newton willingly became involved in the horrific slave trade, eventually captaining two slave ships.

Fortunately, God's Spirit can transform the hardest heart. After a series of near-death experiences, Newton placed his faith in Jesus. From that point on, God's Spirit changed his life. He began to read and study the Bible. His vulgarity, insubordination, drinking, and gambling quickly came to an end. Though it took a few years, he gradually removed himself from the slave trade and became a gifted pastor. He turned his creativity to righteous ends and wrote the most famous hymn of all time, *Amazing Grace*. And toward the end of his life, he dedicated himself to the abolitionist movement, fighting publicly against the slave trade. Now, hundreds of years later, the world remembers John Newton not as a vulgar slave trader but as a gracious and humble pastor, writer, and advocate of freedom. Such is the radical transformation available to all who trust in Jesus![2]

## MAKE IT REAL

9. Where do you turn for strength when life is hard? Use the following exercise to help you answer that question.

   • When I'm angry, stressed, or tired, I respond by . . .

- When I'm tempted, I respond by . . .

- When I'm suffering for my faith, I respond by . . .

10. Many believers don't think to turn to the Lord for help when life is hard. If that includes you, what keeps you from turning to God? Why do you seek help from other sources?

What bold steps of faith is God calling you to take through the strength provided by His Spirit? If you're not sure, take some time to pray and ask God before working through this activity.

### Steps of Faith

☐  Is there a person or group that God is calling you to share the gospel with? If so, list their names:

☐ Is there a sinful part of your life that God is calling you to leave behind? If so, what practical steps do you need to take to find victory? Who will hold you accountable to take these steps?

☐ Is there a person you need to forgive? If so, when will you take that step?

☐ Is there a person you need to ask forgiveness from? If so, when will you take that step?

☐ Is there a sacrifice you need to make in order to serve the Lord (time, money, reputation, relationship)? If so, who will hold you accountable to follow through?

# MEMORIZE

Review the memory verses from the previous lessons. Then memorize Galatians 5:16 (ESV):

**But I say, walk by the Spirit, and you will not gratify the desires of the flesh.**

Now that you've had the chance to think through the steps of faith God has called you to take, spend some time sharing what you discovered with your group or accountability partner. Pray together for God to strengthen your faith and courage. Just as Peter was transformed through the power of the Holy Spirit, so God can transform you and use you like Peter to make an eternal impact on this world. All you have to do is trust and obey Him through the power of His Spirit.

# Leader's Guide

WE'RE GLAD THAT you've decided to lead your group through this study of the life of Peter. We pray that God will use this study to transform you and the students in your group into more faithful servants of Him. The Word of God really can change us for the better when we study it together and challenge each other to obey it.

The degree to which a small group understands and applies the Scriptures ultimately depends on the work of the Holy Spirit. However, the leader has a critical role in helping the group listen carefully to God's Word. Your role, then, is to constantly point your group back to the Scriptures and to challenge them to understand and apply it. As you guide your group through the main passages of Scripture and additional verses of study, be sure participants each have a Bible so they can fully engage with the Word.

## LESSON FORMAT

Each lesson of this study is broken down into four major sections (this format is loosely based on the inductive Bible study methodology outlined in *Living by the Book*, by Howard and William Hendricks[1]):

**Introduction/Need:** Every lesson begins with an opening story designed to stir interest in the subject and to relate the main point of the passage to a real-life situation. Following the written introduction, we have included a few questions to provoke some initial thought about the week's topic. Our goal in this section is simply to help the group see the need to study the passage and to introduce perhaps one or two ways in which the passage might be personally relevant.

**Look It Over:** This section is designed to stimulate observation directly from the text. The purpose of these questions is not to inquire about the *meaning* of the text (the next section will accomplish that goal), but instead just to observe what the passage actually *says*. As a leader, you'll want to continually challenge the group to ground their observations in the biblical text. One temptation at this stage will be for you or other group members to jump ahead to application. For example, if the passage talks about Peter's struggle with faith, it might be tempting at the outset to say, "Peter struggled to believe in Jesus' promise to protect him. What promises of God do you struggle to believe?" That's an application question; save those sorts of questions for the final section, "Make It Real." Instead, at this stage focus on questions related to the text itself: "What promises did Peter struggle to believe in this passage?" or "How did Jesus respond to Peter's lack of faith?" By studying the passage carefully, your group will be better prepared to understand and apply it.

**Think It Through:** This portion of the study is designed to take students deeper into the text through the process of interpretation. Sometimes we need to answer difficult questions before we can apply the text. For instance, the world of the Bible was quite different from our own. As a result, you might need to walk your group through a bit of background study or look up a few cross-references. Where necessary, we've provided dialogue boxes with critical information to help you in this process. For example, in the first lesson it helps to know the basics of fishing in the ancient world so we can understand the significance of Peter's first encounter with Jesus on the Sea of Galilee. Continue to resist the temptation to apply the text at this point; instead, help your group understand what it means (not what it means *to you or to the students* but what it actually means *in light of the original context*).

**Make It Real:** The final section of each lesson is designed to encourage personal application of the text. Every passage of Scripture, even those that seem the strangest to us today, contains principles that are timeless and can be applied to our lives. To that end, we've provided questions and exercises to prompt the students to reflect on their own lives, identify where they are falling short, and make a specific plan for growth. Don't let your group members leave their applications general ("I will be more thankful to God"); help them make specific, concrete plans ("I will grow in thankfulness by spending at least five minutes a day each day this week writing down specific things I am thankful to God for"). As the leader, consider organizing group activities for some of the applications. Students (especially young men) often connect with one another and learn best in an active setting, so you might plan service projects, road trips, or other similar events to help with the application process. We also encourage group accountability. Don't allow the applications to be forgotten after the discussion for each lesson, but instead return to them in subsequent weeks to help your group hold one another accountable.

At the end of each lesson we have included a memory verse. We encourage you to have your group members recite these each week. However, if memorizing all of the verses is too overwhelming, pick one or two and focus on them throughout the course of the study.

## STRUCTURING YOUR TIME

Depending on the topic, the composition of your group, and their level of preparation, your group time might be structured in several different ways. We recommend that you allow at least an hour for your group meetings, and more time if possible. Assuming that your group has about an hour to meet, here is a suggested timeline (adjust this proportionately if you have more or less time each week):

- *5–10 minutes:* Welcome and prayer
- *5–10 minutes:* Introduction/Need
- *10–15 minutes:* Look It Over
- *15–20 minutes:* Think It Through
- *10–15 minutes:* Make It Real

We recognize that it is often challenging to answer all of the questions in your allotted time. If one question or concept generates a great deal of discussion, it's not always wise to end the dialogue simply to move on to the next question. As the leader, use your discretion to determine whether to allow a "rabbit trail" or to gently encourage the group to move on to a different topic. Consider carefully whether a particular discussion is the most productive use of time for the entire group. If an issue is troubling one member more than the others, offer to meet with him or her individually at a different time. That will allow you to continue with the study in a way that meets the needs of all members.

Nothing energizes a Bible study like challenging questions. Though we've included many questions in the book, we encourage you to go beyond them. Brainstorm questions of your own from the passage to ask your group. Include "devil's advocate" questions where you take a counterposition and force your group to defend their views from Scripture. Many students, especially guys, love debate, so don't hesitate to dial up the tension in your meetings!

If your group has not prepared ahead of time, begin by reading the lesson's passage with them and encouraging them to verbally make observations. You might want to provide some initial observations and thoughts on the passage for your group just to get them started. You can write their observations on a dry-erase board, project them onto a screen, or have the group members write them in their own books. After spending a few minutes observing, challenge them to answer the most critical questions from "Think It Through" on the spot. Finally, prompt them to think through how they might apply the text this coming week.

Most important, do not skip the "Make It Real" portion of the study in the interest of time. Ultimately, the effectiveness of a Bible study is measured by the impact it has on the group members' lives, not by the knowledge it generates. If you are short on time, move quickly through the "Look It Over" and "Think It Through" sections so you have time to discuss applications.

# THEMES AND KEY QUESTIONS FOR EACH WEEK

Though there are countless lessons to learn from Peter's life, our primary focus in this study is on how Peter challenges us to seek true, lasting greatness by following Jesus Christ. Greatness comes to those who allow God to transform them just as He transformed Peter from an ambitious, self-centered fisherman into a selfless, powerful leader. If God can transform a man as reckless as Peter, then He can transform any of us! But to experience God's power, we must be willing to set aside our selfish ambitions and worldly desires and, instead, follow the example of service, humility, and suffering set by our Savior.

Each lesson of the study contributes to that idea in a different way. Here are the themes and critical questions to answer for each lesson of the study:

**Lesson 1:** This lesson focuses more on Jesus than on Peter. Your primary goal is to help your group understand (1) who Jesus is—God the Son in human flesh, and (2) what Jesus offers—forgiveness of sins to all who believe in Him. Use the download activity to get a sense of who in your group is a believer and who is not. Plan to spend extra time before and after your meetings with those who are not believers to share the gospel with them and discuss objections they may have. For those who are believers, questions 7 and 8 are particularly important. Until we understand how serious it is to sin against an infinitely holy, almighty God, we will never appreciate how wonderful His grace and forgiveness really are! Note in question 7 that by "sinful," Peter doesn't simply mean that he's done a couple of bad things. "Sinful" is who Peter is by nature: a rebel against God who continually sins and, therefore, deserves God's wrath (His righteous punishment of sin). So for question 8, yes, of course Peter should be fearful! He's in the presence of the power of God (see the dialogue box on fishing to see how great a miracle this is) and God's response to sin is always wrath. Romans 1:18 and Ephesians 2:1-3 may be helpful to prove these points. Also, Matthew 5:21-22,27-28,48 will prove beyond a shadow of a doubt that all of us, like Peter, are sinful!

That's why Jesus' words in Luke 5:10 are so meaningful. Though Peter deserves punishment from Jesus, Jesus instead gives him peace ("don't be afraid") and an eternally significant purpose in life ("you will catch men"). See also Ephesians 2:4-10.

**Lesson 2:** This lesson focuses on Jesus' mission for His followers: to boldly share the gospel even if it results in suffering. This is the answer to question 1, though it could be expressed in many different ways (for example, "share the gospel," "tell people about Jesus," "glorify God" [which you do by telling people about Him!]). Use this to see whether your group members understand and embrace that mission or not. If not, help them identify what "mission" they are living for (for example, "to be happy," "to make money," and so forth) and why it falls short of the mission Jesus offers us. Question 10 reveals just one of the reasons why Jesus' mission is best: because it results in eternal reward! The believer who faithfully serves Jesus in this life gets to rule with Jesus in the next life (see Revelation 2:26-27)! If you desire to go deeper on that subject, turn to 2 Timothy 2:11-13. The four lines of this poem are parallel. The first and fourth tell us why our salvation is absolutely secure: because it rests on God's faithfulness, not ours. The second and third tell us why we should be faithful to God: because if we're faithful even when it results in suffering, then we'll rule with Him; if we're not, then He will deny us this privilege (not eternal life). Finally, spend some time discussing the "Make It Real" section. Does each member of your group know how to share the gospel (it's summarized in the last sentence of Same Mission, New Message on page 31)? Have your group members list specific people they can share it with and spend time praying for opportunities.

**Lesson 3:** This lesson focuses on faith. The discussion on page 35 about faith as both a one-time event bringing justification and an on-going process bringing growth is particularly important to cover. Matthew 14 is about the latter. Peter's already been justified through faith in Jesus. Now he needs to grow in trust, learning to depend ever more fully on the promises of Jesus. That's the goal for the members of your group as well: to walk in greater faith, taking bolder steps of obedience to serve and glorify Jesus. To that end, reserve time to discuss question 11 at length. Look up these promises and help your group realize that these are God's promises to *us*. How would our lives look different if we *really* believed that God would do for us all that He promises to do in these verses? In the download activity, encourage your group to hold each member accountable to follow through on the steps he or she has indicated (include yourself in that accountability!).

**Lesson 4:** There are two key ideas to focus on in this lesson. The first, based on Matthew 16:13-20, is to understand what it means that Jesus is the *Christ*. Discuss what it would have been like to be a first-century Jew living under centuries of oppression, without any way to gain your freedom or improve your life. Your only hope would have been God's promise to send His Christ. If you have time, read Isaiah 9:2-7 and 11:1-10 to see the hope Israel placed in their Messiah. Unfortunately, after so many years of oppression, most of the Israelites focused their attention predominantly on the military aspects of the Messiah prophecy. That's the focus of question 6—they weren't expecting a Messiah cloaked in humility and talking about service. Your second focus in this lesson is Peter's blunder in Matthew 16:21-27. Peter still pinned his hopes on earthly fame and fortune. He expected his allegiance to God's Christ to bring monetary reward. So when Jesus predicts suffering and death, Peter revolts! We are prone to the same error when we place our earthly desires and ambitions above God's priorities. Focus some time on questions 10 and 11 because growth in contentment is the best way to avoid Peter's error.

**Lesson 5:** This lesson targets our struggle with pride and selfishness. Spend some time really discussing question 2. Pride and selfishness are so insidious! They're ingrained in our culture and our sin nature. In fact, you can make a case that pride and selfishness are at the root of every sin we commit. Spend time also on question 5. It's nearly impossible to resist pride until we adopt Jesus' definition of true greatness—that greatness comes through serving and promoting others above yourself. Then look at question 8—this is the key to the whole lesson. If Jesus, the infinite, omnipotent Creator, was willing to sacrifice His rights, desires, and even His life for us, then how can we not willingly sacrifice our rights and desires for one another? You may want to read Philippians 2:5-11 as you discuss this question. Finally, as the leader of the group, put some thought into the second download activity. We tend to learn best when we do something together and this is a great lesson to apply as a group. If you need ideas, ask a staff member, elder, or deacon at your church, or call up a reputable local charity group.

**Lesson 6:** This lesson looks at the darkest moments of Peter's life to help us understand how sin and temptation trip us up. Questions 6, 7, and 8 are especially important. Question 6 reminds us that we have an Enemy actively seeking our destruction. If time permits, have your group read John 8:44, Ephesians 4:26-27, Ephesians 6:11-17, and 1 Peter 5:8-9 to see some of the tactics Satan uses against us and how we can fight back. Question 7 is crucial to understanding salvation. Read the passage from Romans 8 and focus on the phrase "anything else in all creation" in verse 39. Even if my faith fails, I cannot separate myself from God's saving love because I am part of His creation. Our salvation rests securely in God's hands, not ours. For question 8, focus on verses 5, 10, and 11 in Isaiah 53. Only by suffering death could Jesus pave the way for our salvation (see also Romans 3:23-26 and Hebrews 9:22). Finally, leave plenty of time for the "Make It Real" section. For question 10, it may be helpful to read 1 John 1:5–2:2. Note how confession, which means to agree with God that what we did was sin, restores us to fellowship with God. Sin did not cost us our eternal life, but it did prevent us from enjoying God's presence and power in our lives (He can't "hang out" with those who walk in the darkness of sin). Confession fixes that.

**Lesson 7:** This lesson is designed to give us hope by demonstrating that God's grace is limitless. If His grace can restore Peter after his betrayal and Samson after his lust, then it can restore any of us who've fallen in sin. We are not beyond hope! Spend time on questions 2 and 3 to see if your group members really grasp the grace of God. Do they understand and believe that God always loves us no matter what we do? Or do they see God as a hockey referee who throws us in the penalty box when we sin? That's not God. Question 7 is designed to help us understand the radical extent of God's forgiveness. He "forgets" our sins. Now God is omniscient—He knows all things past, present, and future, so "forget" doesn't mean "unable to remember," it means "choosing not to remember." God never allows the memory of our forgiven sins to occupy His mind. Question 8 is challenging and meant to generate debate. It's one of the most difficult questions that elder boards struggle with. The key is the phrase "above reproach"—the leaders of the church need to have lived such godly lives in the eyes of the community that no one could legitimately charge them with a major sin. When a leader does fail publicly and seriously but then repents, it may be best for him or her to serve in a less-visible support role in order to protect the reputation of Christ in the community. Spend time talking about what it means to love the Lord (questions 10 and 12). We use that phrase often without thinking about what it really means. Biblically, it's less about a feeling and more about an action: obedience. Finally, use the download activity to help your group members move toward future leadership in the church. Ideally, one or more of them will soon be ready to lead a small group of their own. Consider letting one of these individuals lead all or part of the next group meeting to give them practice in leadership. Remember, the ultimate goal of a small group leader is to raise up other leaders!

**Lesson 8:** Though the passages in Acts are long, the story of Peter's transformation is inspiring and powerful. This lesson focuses on the agent in that transformation: the Holy Spirit. All believers have been indwelt by the Spirit. But to fully experience His power we must learn to walk with Him in dependence and obedience. Focus on question 6. Of the cross-references included in that question, Galatians 5 and Philippians 2 are the most helpful because they spell out exactly what our part is in this process of transformation. Note that in Galatians 5, "live by" in verse 16 (or "walk by" in some translations) is parallel to "led by" in verse 18. It means to dependently follow the leading of the Spirit much like a child dependently follows hand in hand the leading of a parent. When we let the Spirit lead our lives, the result is His fruit (see verses 22-23) produced through us for the benefit of others and us. Philippians 2 gives us the second, parallel step: continually obey. As we choose to obey God daily, God works in us through His Spirit to give us both the ability to obey and the desire to obey (literally: "to *will [desire]* and to *work* for His good pleasure" [verse 13, NASB, emphasis added]). Finally, spend time on the download activity. This is a great way to end your study of Peter's life. Just like him, we are each called to take bold, risky steps of faith. Challenge each individual in your group to commit to one or more specific steps of faith to take in the coming weeks.

## "BE MY WITNESSES . . . TO THE ENDS OF THE EARTH!"

May God use this study to inspire and empower you and your group to be witnesses for Jesus in your home, in your community, and throughout the world! We're confident that His Spirit will be at work in your group as you diligently study and faithfully apply His Word. For further resources, feel free to look at Grace Bible Church's website, www.grace-bible.org, or contact NavPress at www.navpress.com. And don't forget to check out the other studies in the ORDINARY GREATNESS series.

# Notes

## LESSON 1: DIVINITY IN DISGUISE

1. Gene Weingarten, "Pearls Before Breakfast," *Washington Post,* April 8, 2007, http://www.washingtonpost.com/wp-dyn/content/article/2007/04/04/AR2007040401721.html.
2. Craig S. Keener, *A Commentary on the Gospel of Matthew: A Socio-Rhetorical Commentary* (Grand Rapids, MI: Eerdmans, 2009), 152.
3. Dick Sternberg and North American Fishing Club, *The Ultimate Guide to Freshwater Fishing* (Chaska, MN: Publishing Solutions, 2003), 12–13.

## LESSON 2: YOUR MISSION, SHOULD YOU CHOOSE TO ACCEPT IT

1. Elisabeth Elliot, *Shadow of the Almighty: The Life and Testament of Jim Elliot* (Peabody, MA: Hendrickson, 2008), 19.
2. "Ignatius of Antioch: Letters," *Wikipedia,* http://en.wikipedia.org/wiki/Ignatius_of_Antioch.
3. Elliot, 15.

## LESSON 4: TWO STEPS FORWARD, TWO STEPS BACK

1. "Oops . . . ," Pro Football Hall of Fame, http://www.profootballhof.com/history/story.aspx?story_id=2092.

## LESSON 5: THE LAST ARE FIRST

1. "Schwerer Gustav," *Wikipedia,* http://en.wikipedia.org/wiki/Schwerer_Gustav.
2. John F. Walvoord, Roy B. Zuck, and Dallas Theological Seminary, *The Bible Knowledge Commentary: An Exposition of the Scriptures* (Wheaton, IL: Victor, 1983), 146.
3. Warren W. Wiersbe, *The Bible Exposition Commentary* (Wheaton, IL: Victor, 1996).

4. Johannes P. Louw and Eugene A. Nida, *Greek-English Lexicon of the New Testament*, vol. 1 (New York: United Bible Societies, 1999), 459.
5. Galvin Childress, *Opening up Luke's Gospel* (Leominster, UK: Day One, 2006).
6. Leslie Bruce and Judith Newman, "How the Kardashians Made $65 Million Last Year," *The Hollywood Reporter,* February 16, 2011, http://www.hollywoodreporter.com/news/how-kardashians-made-65-million-100349.

## LESSON 8: A NEW MAN

1. "The Jarvik 2000: The First Lifetime-Use Patient," Jarvik Heart, http://www.jarvikheart.com/basic.asp?id=63; Kathy Watson, "Patient Sets World Record for Living with Heart Assist Device," Texas Heart Institute, July 6, 2007, http://www.texasheart.org/AboutUs/News/Lucky7_device_07_06_07.cfm.
2. "John Newton," *Wikipedia,* http://en.wikipedia.org/wiki/John_Newton; "Amazing Grace," *Wikipedia,* http://en.wikipedia.org/wiki/Amazing_Grace.

## LEADER'S GUIDE

1. Howard and William Hendricks, *Living by the Book* (Chicago: Moody, 1991).

# About the Authors

**Blake Jennings, Matt Morton, and Brian Fisher** serve together at Grace Bible Church in College Station, Texas. GBC is a multisite church of four thousand people located near Texas A&M University. Because of the church's focus on the next generation of spiritual leaders, more than two thousand students attend weekly college worship times and participate in weekly Bible studies, discipleship, and summer missions opportunities.

**Blake** is the teaching pastor of GBC's Southwood Campus. He graduated from Dallas Theological Seminary and Texas A&M University. He and his wife, Julie, are the proud parents of Gracie and Luke.

**Matt** is the college pastor of GBC's Anderson Campus. He graduated from Dallas Theological Seminary and Texas A&M University. He and his wife, Shannon, have three wonderful children.

**Brian** serves as the senior pastor of GBC. He holds a master's degree and a doctorate from Dallas Theological Seminary and is a graduate of Texas A&M University. He is married to Tristie. They have two beautiful children.